PHOTO
PUZZLE HUNT

The Ultimate
Spot-The-Differences Challenge

PHOTO
PUZZLE HUNT

The Ultimate
Spot-The-Differences Challenge

Christine Reguigne

STERLING

New York / London
www.sterlingpublishing.com

Library of Congress Cataloging-in-Publication Data available

6 8 10 9 7

Published by Sterling Publishing Co., Inc.
387 Park Avenue South, New York, NY 10016
© 2007 by Christine Reguigne

This book is comprised of materials from the following Sterling titles:
Spot the Differences © 2003 by Christine Reguigne
Spot the Differences: Vehicles © 2004 by Christine Reguigne

Distributed in Canada by Sterling Publishing
c/o Canadian Manda Group, 165 Dufferin Street,
Toronto, Ontario, Canada M6K 3H6
Distributed in the United Kingdom by GMC Distribution Services,
Castle Place, 166 High Street, Lewes, East Sussex, England BN7 1XU
Distributed in Australia by Capricorn Link (Australia) Pty. Ltd.
P.O. Box 704, Windsor, NSW 2756, Australia

Printed in China
All rights reserved

Sterling ISBN-13: 978-1-4027-5178-3
ISBN-10: 1-4027-5178-8

For information about custom editions, special sales, premium and
corporate purchases, please contact Sterling Special Sales
Department at 800-805-5489 or specialsales@sterlingpublishing.com.

TABLE OF CONTENTS

TABLE OF CONTENTS

INTRODUCTION

Do you have a knack for being detail-oriented? Test your skills with these beautifully photographed puzzles meant to challenge your perception. Has something disappeared from one picture to the next? Do you notice a hair out of place? You'll have to have an uncannily keen eye to take this puzzle hunt challenge. Choose among images in a variety of themes – from travel and seasons, to animals and vehicles – and discover if you have the skills to spot all of the differences.

Good luck!

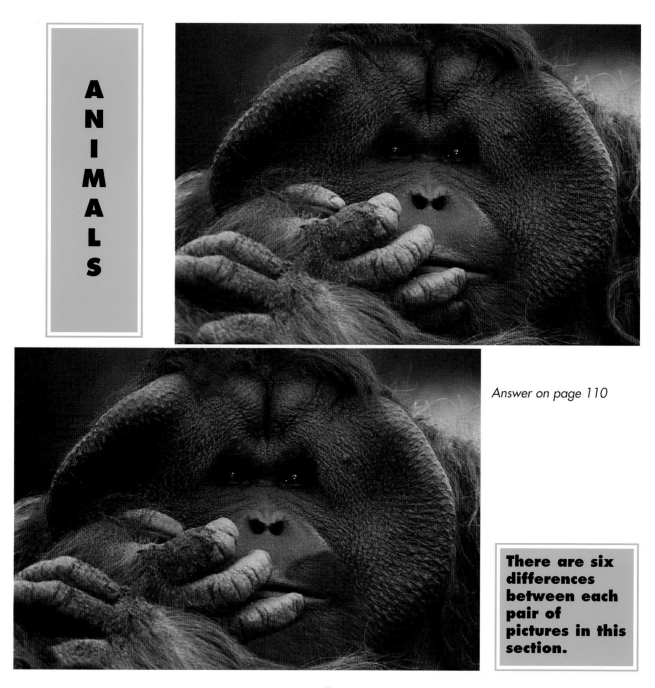

ANIMALS

Answer on page 110

There are six
differences
between each
pair of
pictures in this
section.

Answer on page 112

Answer on page 115

Answer on page 117

Answer on page 120

Answer on page 122

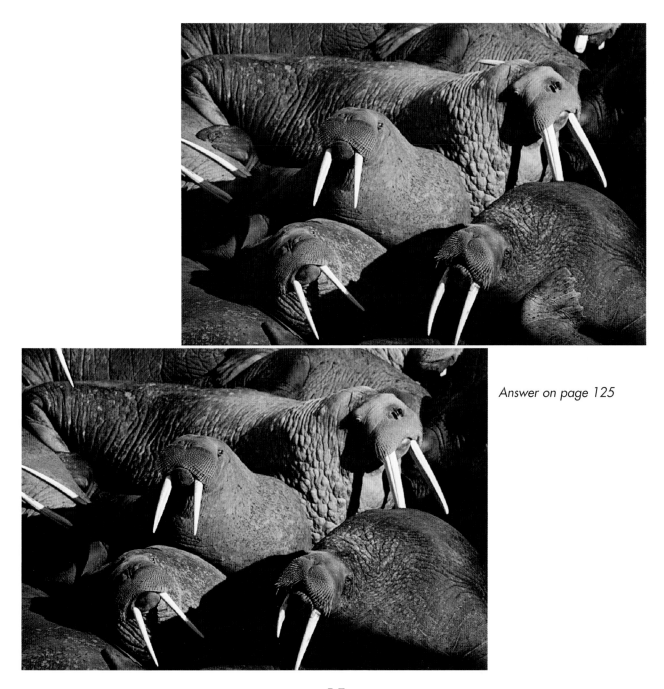

Answer on page 125

Answer on page 127

Answer on page 130

Answer on page 132

Answer on page 110

Answer on page 113

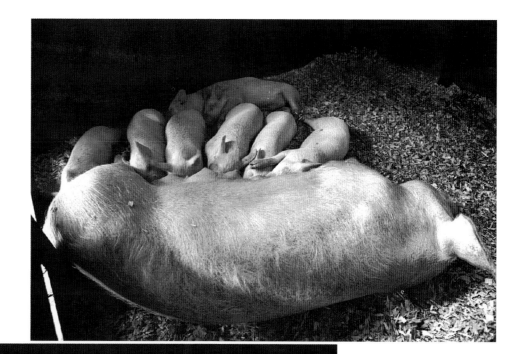

Answer on page 115

Answer on page 118

Answer on page 120

• **23** •

Answer on page 123

Answer on page 125

Answer on page 128

Answer on page 130

Answer on page 133

TRAVEL

Answer on page 111

There are eight differences between each pair of pictures in this section.

Answer on page 113

Answer on page 116

Answer on page 118

Answer on page 121

• **33** •

Answer on page 123

Answer on page 126

Answer on page 128

Answer on page 131

Answer on page 133

Answer on page 111

Answer on page 114

Answer on page 116

Answer on page 119

SEASONS

Answer on page 121

There are six differences between each pair of pictures in this section.

Answer on page 124

Answer on page 126

Answer on page 129

Answer on page 131

Answer on page 134

Answer on page 112

Answer on page 114

Answer on page 117

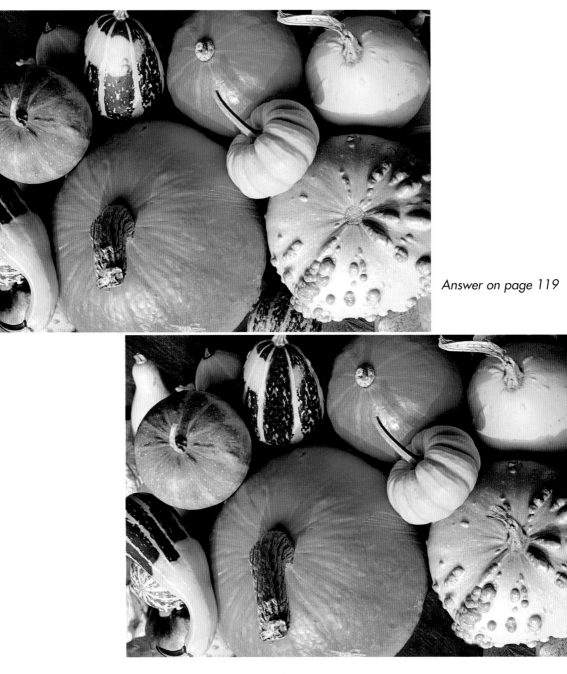

Answer on page 119

Answer on page 122

Answer on page 124

Answer on page 127

Answer on page 129

Answer on page 132

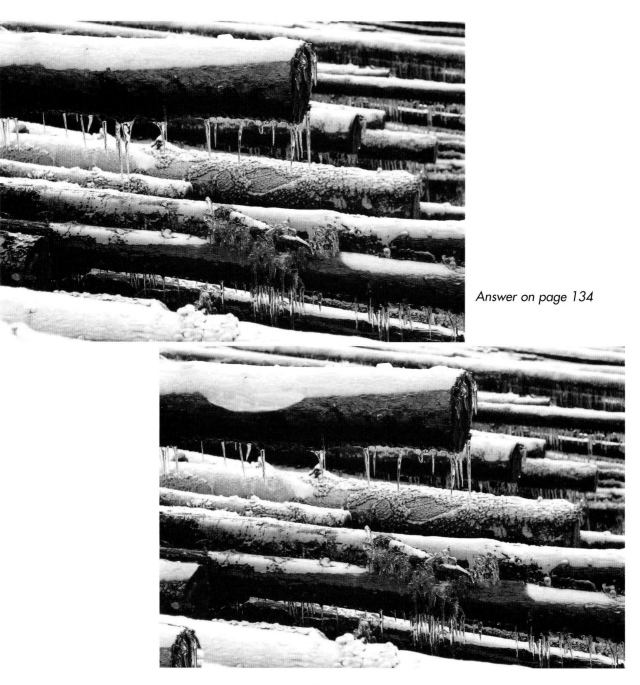

Answer on page 134

Answer on page 159

There are six
differences
between each
pair of pictures
in this section.

Answer on page 136

Answer on page 139

Answer on page 141

Answer on page 144

Answer on page 146

Answer on page 149

Answer on page 151

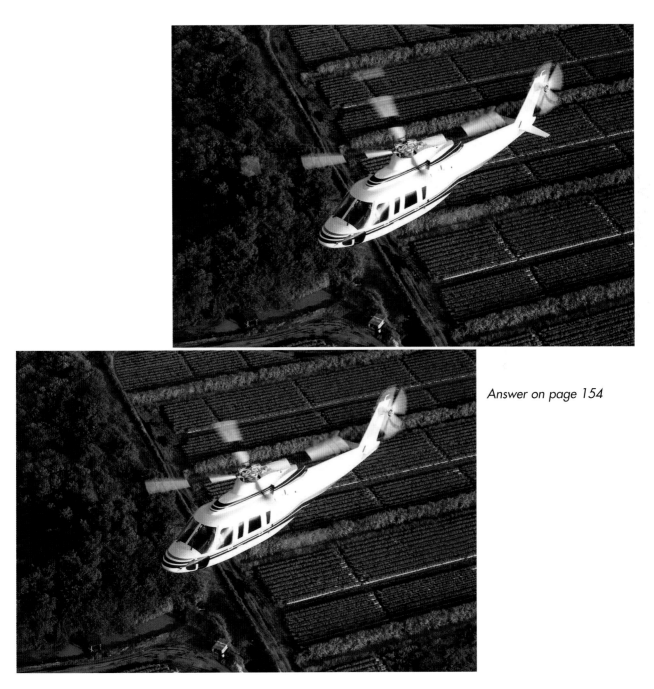

Answer on page 154

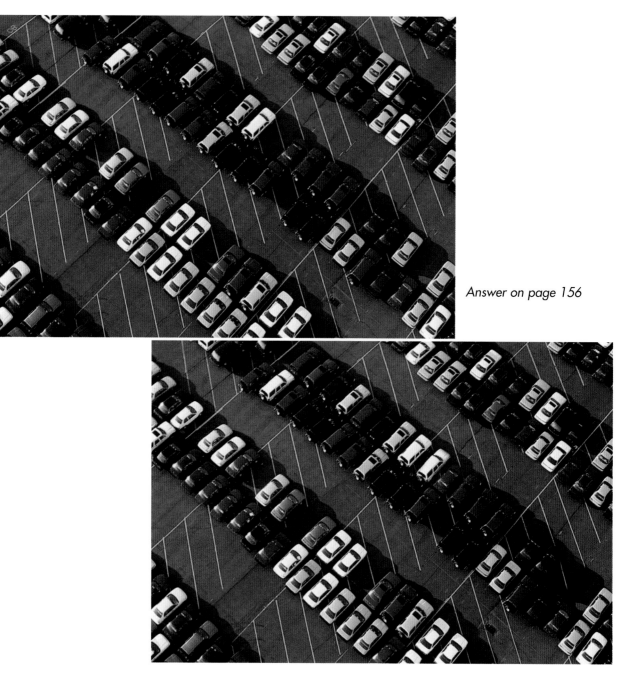

Answer on page 156

Answer on page 159

Answer on page 137

Answer on page 139

Answer on page 142

Answer on page 144

Answer on page 147

Answer on page 149

Answer on page 152

Answer on page 154

Answer on page 157

Answer on page 135

Answer on page 137

Answer on page 140

Answer on page 142

Answer on page 145

Answer on page 147

Answer on page 150

Answer on page 152

Answer on page 155

Answer on page 157

Answer on page 135

Answer on page 138

Answer on page 140

Answer on page 143

Answer on page 145

Answer on page 148

Answer on page 150

Answer on page 153

Answer on page 155

Answer on page 158

Answer on page 136

Answer on page 138

Answer on page 141

Answer on page 143

Answer on page 146

Answer on page 148

Answer on page 151

Answer on page 153

Answer on page 156

Answer on page 158

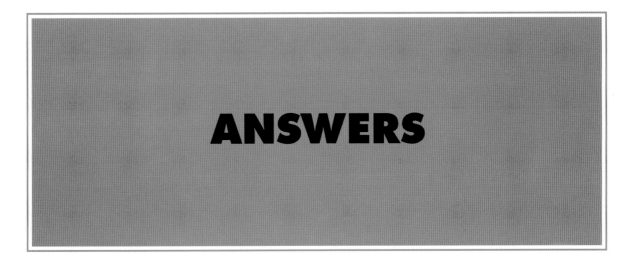

ANSWERS

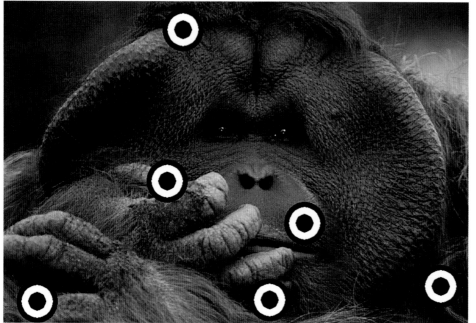

Puzzle page 9

Puzzle page 19

Puzzle page 29

Puzzle page 39

Puzzle page 49

Puzzle page 10

Puzzle page 20

Puzzle page 30

Puzzle page 40

Puzzle page 50

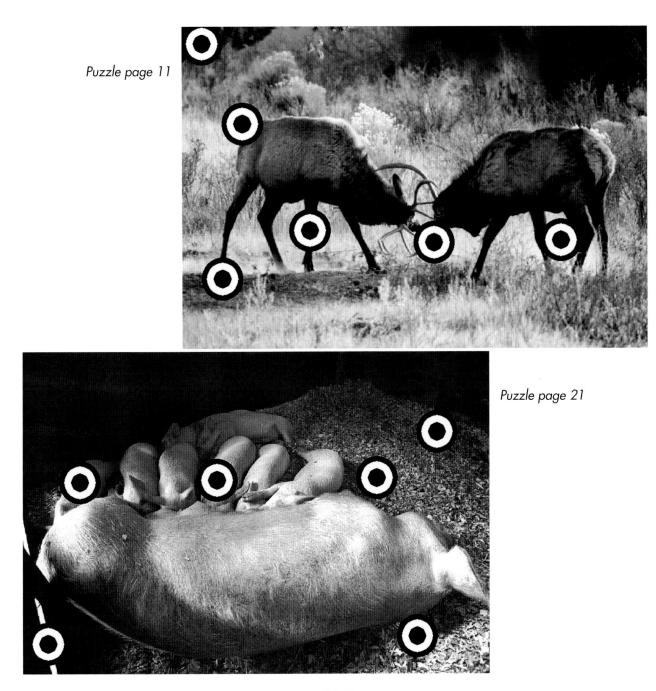

Puzzle page 11

Puzzle page 21

Puzzle page 31

Puzzle page 41

Puzzle page 51

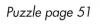

Puzzle page 12

Puzzle page 22

Puzzle page 32

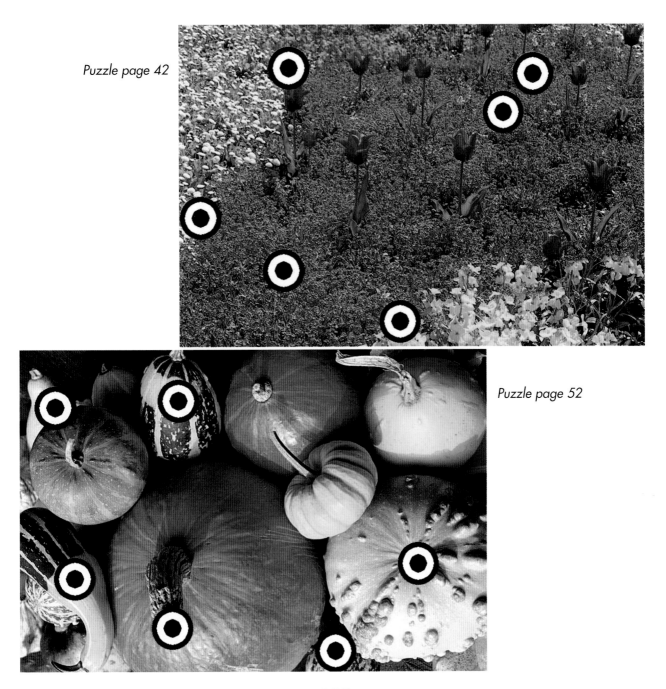

Puzzle page 42

Puzzle page 52

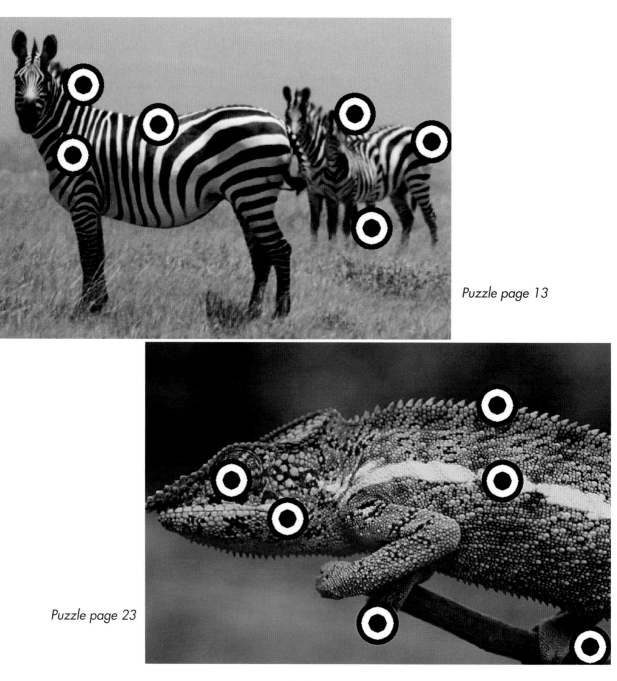

Puzzle page 13

Puzzle page 23

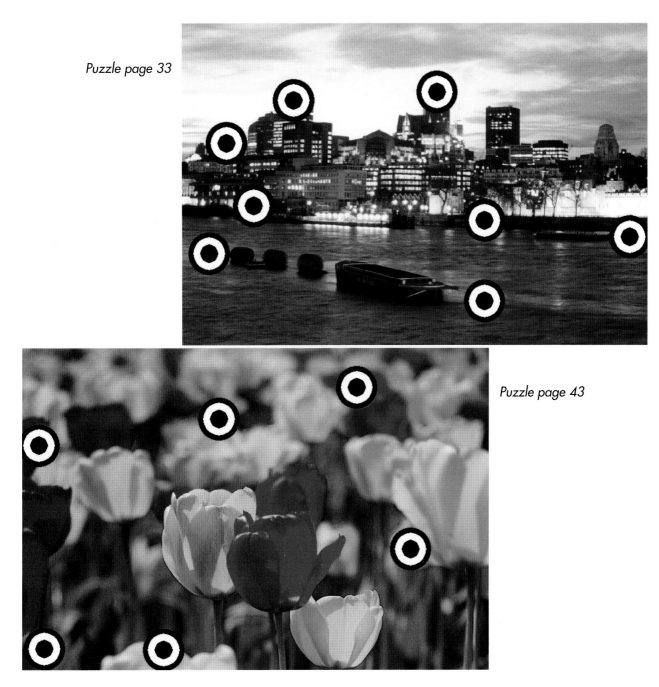

Puzzle page 33

Puzzle page 43

Puzzle page 53

Puzzle page 14

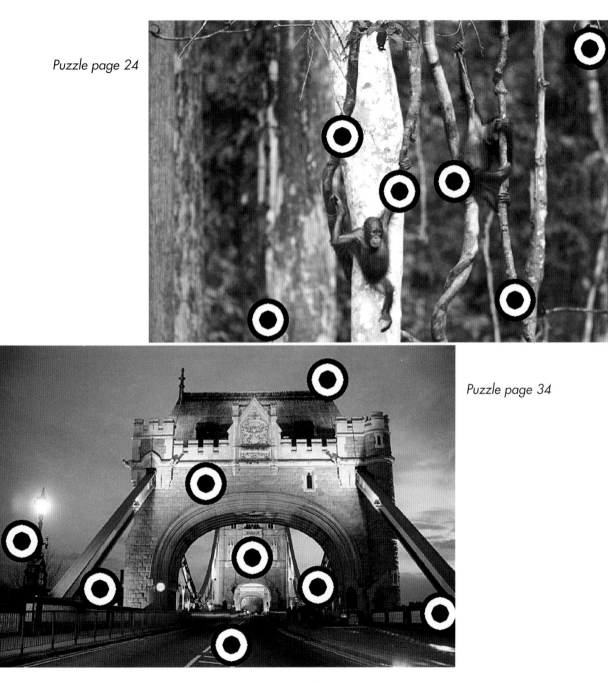

Puzzle page 24

Puzzle page 34

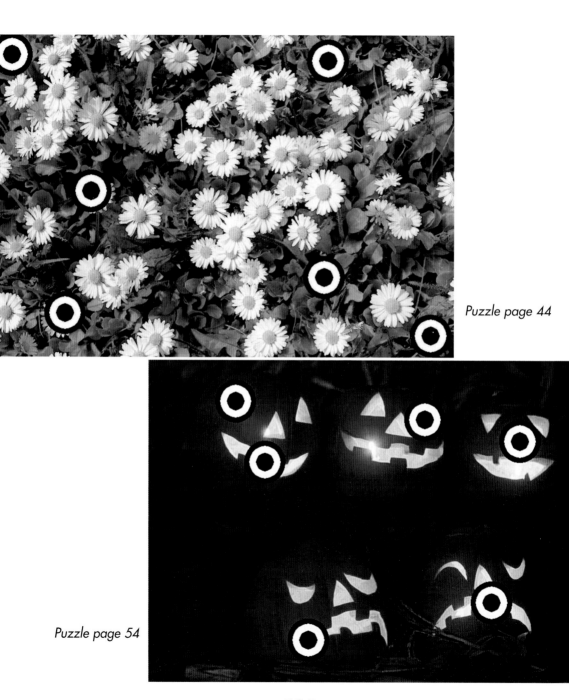

Puzzle page 44

Puzzle page 54

Puzzle page 15

Puzzle page 25

Puzzle page 35

Puzzle page 45

Puzzle page 55

Puzzle page 16

Puzzle page 26

Puzzle page 36

Puzzle page 46

Puzzle page 56

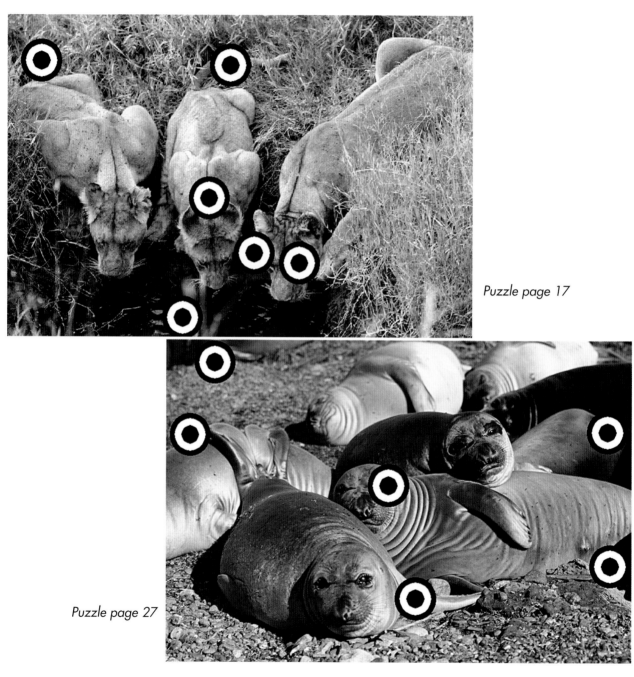

Puzzle page 17

Puzzle page 27

Puzzle page 37

Puzzle page 47

Puzzle page 57

Puzzle page 18

Puzzle page 28

Puzzle page 38

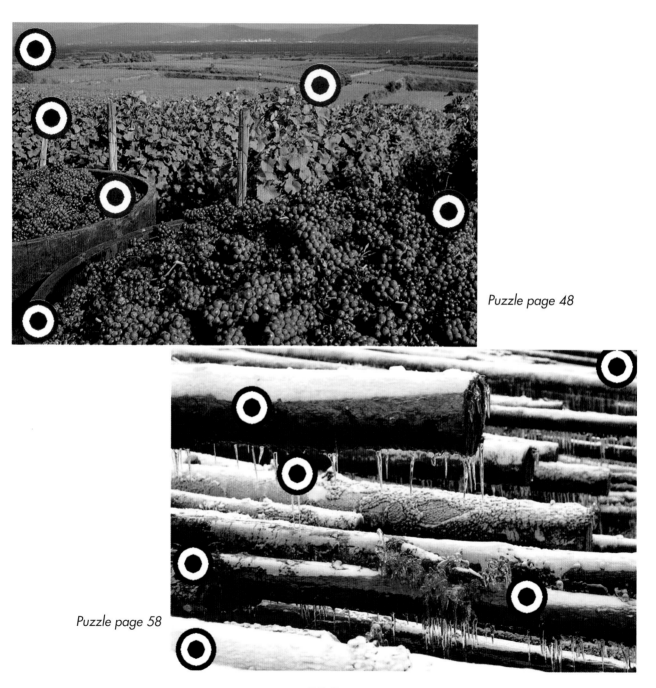

Puzzle page 48

Puzzle page 58

Puzzle page 79

Puzzle page 89

Puzzle page 99

Puzzle page 60

Puzzle page 70

Puzzle page 80

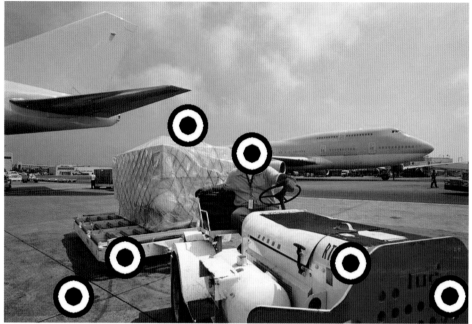

Puzzle page 90

Puzzle page 100

Puzzle page 61

Puzzle page 71

Puzzle page 81

Puzzle page 91

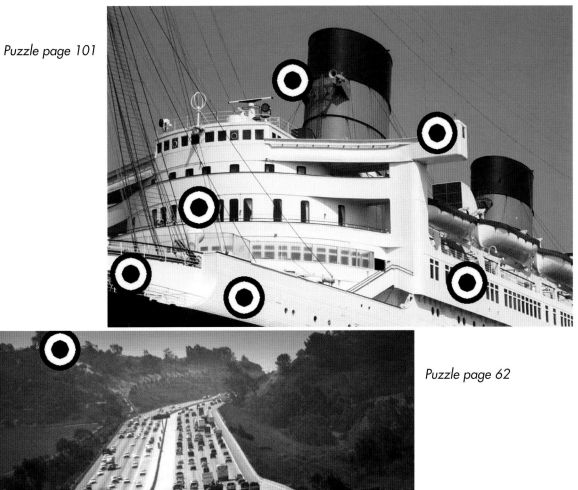

Puzzle page 101

Puzzle page 62

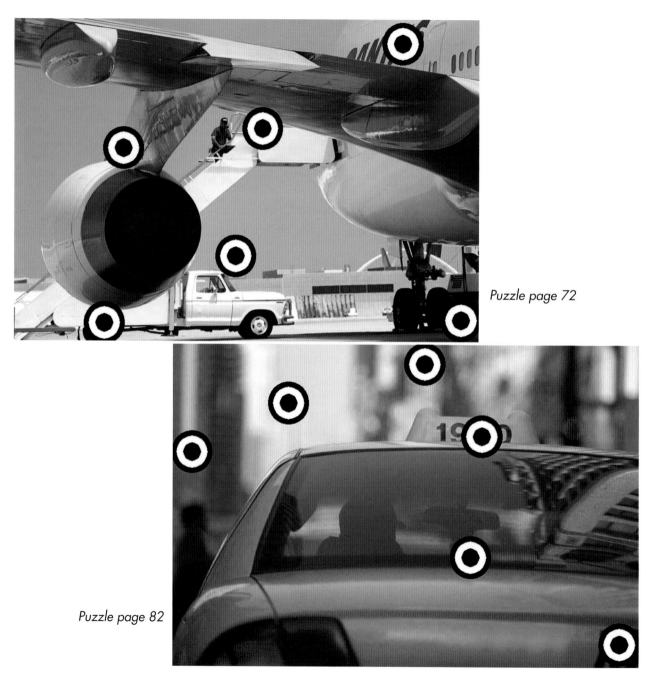

Puzzle page 72

Puzzle page 82

Puzzle page 92

Puzzle page 102

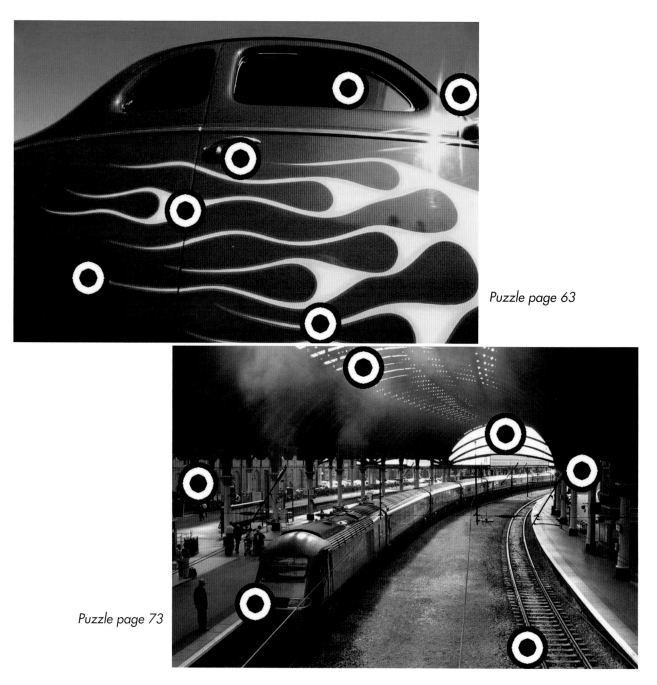

Puzzle page 63

Puzzle page 73

Puzzle page 83

Puzzle page 93

Puzzle page 103

Puzzle page 64

Puzzle page 74

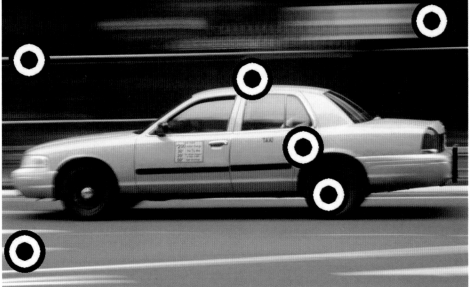

Puzzle page 84

Puzzle page 94

Puzzle page 104

Puzzle page 65

Puzzle page 75

Puzzle page 85

Puzzle page 95

Puzzle page 105

Puzzle page 66

Puzzle page 76

Puzzle page 86

Puzzle page 96

Puzzle page 106

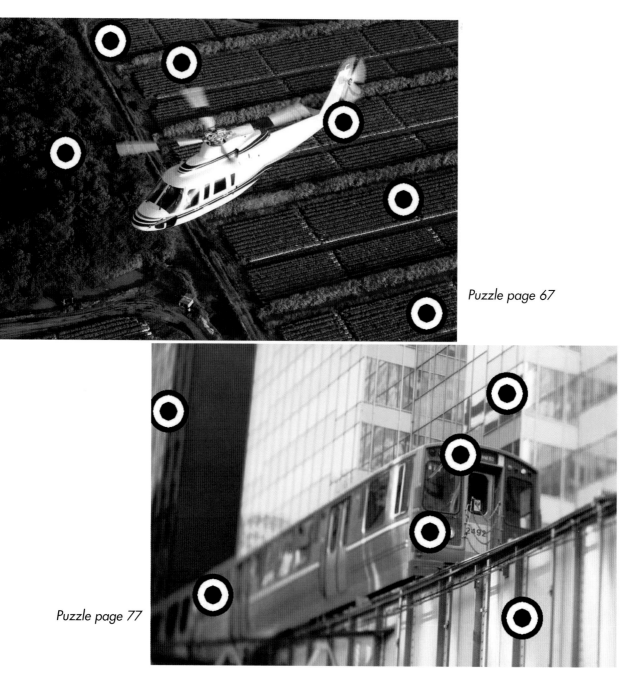

Puzzle page 67

Puzzle page 77

• **154** •

Puzzle page 87

Puzzle page 97

Puzzle page 107

Puzzle page 68

Puzzle page 78

Puzzle page 88

Puzzle page 98

Puzzle page 108

Puzzle page 59

Puzzle page 69

Puzzle from cover